AENEID BOOK VI

by the same author

poetry
DEATH OF A NATURALIST
DOOR INTO THE DARK
WINTERING OUT
NORTH
FIELD WORK
STATION ISLAND
SWEENEY ASTRAY
SWEENEY'S FLIGHT
(with photographs by Rachel Giese)
THE HAW LANTERN
NEW SELECTED POEMS 1966–1987
SEEING THINGS
LAMENTS BY JAN KOCHANOWSKI
(translated with Stanisław Barańczak)
THE SPIRIT LEVEL
OPENED GROUND: POEMS 1966–1996
BEOWULF
ELECTRIC LIGHT
DISTRICT AND CIRCLE
THE TESTAMENT OF CRESSEID & SEVEN FABLES
HUMAN CHAIN
NEW SELECTED POEMS 1988–2013

THE RATTLE BAG
(edited with Ted Hughes)
THE SCHOOL BAG
(edited with Ted Hughes)

prose
PREOCCUPATIONS: SELECTED PROSE 1968–1978
THE GOVERNMENT OF THE TONGUE
THE REDRESS OF POETRY: OXFORD LECTURES
FINDERS KEEPERS: SELECTED PROSE 1971–2001
STEPPING STONES
(with Dennis O'Driscoll)

plays
THE CURE AT TROY
THE BURIAL AT THEBES

AENEID

BOOK VI

translated by

SEAMUS HEANEY

FABER & FABER

First published in 2016
by Faber & Faber Ltd
Bloomsbury House
74–77 Great Russell Street
London WC1B 3DA

Typeset by Faber & Faber Ltd.
Printed by Martins the Printers, Berwick-upon-Tweed

A CIP record for this book is available from the British Library

ISBN 978-0-571-32731-7

4 6 8 10 9 7 5 3

Contents

Translator's Note

THIS TRANSLATION OF *AENEID* VI is neither a 'version' nor a crib: it is more like classics homework, the result of a lifelong desire to honour the memory of my Latin teacher at St Columb's College, Father Michael McGlinchey, about whom I wrote briefly in the prefatory note to *The Golden Bough* (In de Bonnefant and Imprenta de los Trópicos, 1992). The set text for our A level exam in 1957 was *Aeneid* IX but McGlinchey was forever sighing, 'Och, boys, I wish it were Book VI.' Over the years, therefore, I gravitated towards that part of the poem and took special note of it after my father died, since the story it tells is that of Aeneas' journey to meet the shade of his father Anchises in the land of the dead. But the impulse to go ahead with a rendering of the complete book arrived in 2007, as the result of a sequence of poems written to greet the birth of a first granddaughter.

The autobiographical sequence in twelve sections, published in *Human Chain* (2010), was entitled 'Route 110' and plotted incidents from my own life against certain well-known episodes in Book VI: thus a bus inspector's direction of passengers to the bus for Route 110 – the one I often took from Belfast to my home in County Derry – paralleled the moment when Charon directs the shades on board his barge to cross the Styx; and a memory of the wake of a drowned neighbour whose body was not retrieved for three days shadowed the case of Aeneas' drowned, unburied helmsman Palinurus. It was a matter, in other words, of a relatively simple 'mythic method' being employed over the twelve sections. The focus this time, however, was not the meeting of the son with the father, but the vision of future Roman generations with which Book VI ends, specifically the moment on the bank of the River Lethe where we are shown the souls of those about to be reborn and return to life on earth.

'Route 110' also ends with birth and the whole sequence is dedicated to 'one | Whose long wait on the shaded bank has ended'. And so, elated and inspired by having completed the sequence in thanksgiving for that infant birth, and in memory of the man who first turned my ear and temperament to Virgil, I began work on a complete translation of Book VI. Yet as anyone familiar with this work knows, the beginning and middle of that book are alive with poetic and narrative energy, but not so the ending. By the time the story reaches its climax in

Anchises' vision of a glorious Roman race who will issue from Aeneas' marriage with Lavinia, the translator is likely to have moved from inspiration to grim determination: the roll call of generals and imperial heroes, the allusions to variously famous or obscure historical victories and defeats make this part of the poem something of a test for reader and translator alike. But for the sake of the little one whose 'earthlight broke' in late 2006, and the one who sighed for his favourite Virgil in that 1950s classroom, it had to be gone through with.

Michael McGlinchey created an inner literalist who still hunts for the main verb of a sentence and still, to the best of his ability, disentangles the subordinate clauses, although usually nowadays with the help of a crib from the Loeb Library or the old Penguin Classics. Yet nowadays too that sixth form homunculus must contend with a different supervisor, a writer of verse who has things other than literal accuracy on his mind and in his ear: rhythm and metre and lineation, the voice and its pacing, the need for a diction decorous enough for Virgil but not so antique as to sound out of tune with a more contemporary idiom – all the fleeting, fitful anxieties that afflict the literary translator.

SEAMUS HEANEY

AENEID BOOK VI

IN TEARS AS HE SPEAKS, Aeneas loosens out sail
And gives the whole fleet its head, so now at last
They ride ashore on the waves at Euboean Cumae.
There they turn round the ships to face out to sea.
Anchors bite deep, craft are held fast, curved
Sterns cushion on sand, prows frill the beach.
Now a band of young hotbloods vaults quickly out
On to the shore of Italia, some after flint
For the seedling fire it hides in its veins,
Some crashing through woodland thickets, the haunts   10
Of wild beasts, pointing amazed at new rivers.
But Aeneas, devoted as ever, has taken the road
Up towards a fort, the high seat of Apollo,
Then on to a place apart, a vast scaresome cavern,
The Sibyl's deep-hidden retreat. There the god breathes
Into her, overwhelmingly, knowledge and vision,

3

Opening her eyes to the future. Before long
They pass through the golden precincts and groves
Of Diana, the goddess of crossroads.

And now they pause on that hill where Dedalus,   20
At the end of his flight, first fluttered to earth:
He had risked himself to the sky, away and afloat
To the north, through the cold air, unprecedented,
Rowing with wings – which he then dedicated
To you, Phoebus Apollo, there on the spot
Where he landed, and built in your honour
A mighty temple, the doors of it decorated
With scenes in relief.

                First the death of Androgeos.
Then the stricken Athenians, doomed to deliver   30
Seven grown-up sons for sacrifice every year.
There too stood the empty urn, from which
Only now the fatal lots had been drawn.
On the opposite leaf, the land of Knossos
Rising out of the sea: here was the horn-cruel bull
With Pasiphaë under him (a congress
Her cunning arranged), whence would be born
The Minotaur, crossbreed and offspring
Of abominable desire.

                Also shown: 40
The bewildering, intricate maze –
Never got through until Dedalus, out of pity
For infatuated Ariadne,

4

Guided a prince's blind footsteps
With a payout of thread, past every wrong turn
And every dead end he himself had devised
And constructed.
                    In which grand design
You too would figure significantly,
Icarus, had sorrow allowed it. Twice   50
Dedalus tried to model your fall in gold, twice
His hands, the hands of a father, failed him.

The Trojans would have kept standing, fascinated
By all on display, except that just then Achates,
Who'd been sent on ahead, came back accompanied
By the Sibyl, Deiphobe, daughter of Glaucus, priestess
Of Diana and Phoebus. Who addressed the prince:
'This is no time to be standing staring here.
It would be better now to pick out for sacrifice
Seven bullocks from a herd that has not been yoked,   60
And an equal number of properly chosen ewes.'
Having spoken these words to Aeneas (whose men
Are quick to obey her instructions) the priestess
Summons the Trojans into her high inner sanctum.

At Cumae, behind the broad cliff, an enormous cave
Has been quarried: a hundred entrances, a hundred
Wide-open mouths lead in, and out of them scramble
A hundred echoing voices, the Sibyl's responses.
They arrived at that threshold and the vestal cried,

'Now! Now you must ask what your fate is. The god
Is here with us! Apollo!' Her countenance suddenly
Paled and convulsed, hair got dishevelled,
Breast was aheave, heart beating wilder and wilder.
Before their eyes she grows tall, something not mortal
Enters, she is changed by the breath of the god
Breathing through her. 'Aeneas of Troy,' she demands,
'Your vows and your prayers, why do you wait? Pray,
For until you have prayed, the jaws of this cavern
Won't echo or open.' And there she fell silent.
The hardy Trojans feel a cold shiver go through them,
Their prince from the depths of his heart beseeches
The god:

      'Phoebus, you always had pity for Troy
And her troubles, it was you who steadied
Paris's aim and directed the arrow
Into Achilles, you who were pilot
As I entered sea after sea, skirting the coasts
Of distant land masses, remotest Massylia,
The sandbanked Syrtian gulfs. Here then at last
We set foot on Italia that seemed for so long
The unreachable: henceforth let Trojan ill fortune
Be a thing of the past. For now, all you gods
And goddesses, you to whom Troy's name and fame
Gave affront, divine law constrains you
To spare us, the last of its relicts. And you,
Seeress most holy, to whom the future lies open,
Grant what I ask (no more in the end than my fate

6

Has assigned): home ground for my people
In Latium, refuge for our wandering gods
And all Troy ever held sacred. Then to Phoebus   100
Apollo, and Diana, I will set up a temple
In solid marble and inaugurate feast days
In the god's honour. And for you, O all gracious one,
A sanctuary will be established, a vault
Where I shall preserve divinations from lots
And oracles you'll have vouchsafed to my people;
And in your service I shall ordain chosen men.
Yet one thing I ask of you: not to inscribe
Your visions in verse on the leaves
In case they go frolicking off   110
In the wind. Chant them yourself, I beseech you.'
So saying, Aeneas fell silent.

                            Meanwhile the Sibyl,
Resisting possession, storms through the cavern,
In the throes of her struggle with Phoebus
Apollo. But the more she froths at the mouth
And contorts, the more he controls her, commands her
And makes her his creature. Then of their own accord
Those hundred vast tunnel-mouths gape and give vent
To the prophetess's responses: 120

                          'O you who survived,
In the end, the sea's dangers (though worse still await
On the land), you and your Trojans will come
Into your own in Lavinium: have no fear of that.
But the day is one you will rue. I see wars,

7

Atrocious wars, and the Tiber surging with blood.
A second Simois river, a second Xanthus,
A second enemy camp lie ahead. And already
In Latium a second Achilles comes forth, he too
The son of a goddess. Nor will Trojans ever be free   130
Of Juno's harassments, while you, without allies,
Dependent, will go through Italia petitioning
Cities and peoples. And again the cause of such pain
And disaster for Trojans will be as before: a bride
Culled in a host country, an outlander groom.
But whatever disasters befall, do not flinch.
Go all the bolder to face them, follow your fate
To the limit. A road will open to safety
From the last place you would expect: a city of Greeks.'

Thus from her innermost shrine the Sibyl of Cumae   140
Chanted menacing riddles and made the cave echo
With sayings where truths and enigmas were twined
Inextricably, while Apollo reined in her spasms
And curbed her, or sank the spurs in her ribs.

Then as her fit passed away and her raving went quiet,
Heroic Aeneas began: 'No ordeal, O Sibyl, no new
Test can dismay me, for I have foreseen
And foresuffered all. But one thing I pray for
Especially: since here the gate opens, they say,
To the King of the Underworld's realms, and here   150
In these shadowy marshes the Acheron floods

8

To the surface, vouchsafe me one look,
One face-to-face meeting with my dear father.
Point out the road, open the holy doors wide.
On these shoulders I bore him through flames
And a thousand enemy spears. In the thick of fighting
I saved him, and he was at my side then
On all my sea-crossings, battling tempests and tides,
A man in old age, worn out, not meant for duress.
He too it was who half-prayed and half-ordered me   160
To make this approach, to find and petition you.
Wherefore have pity, O most gracious one,
On a son and a father, for you have the power,
You whom Hecate named mistress of wooded Avernus.
If Orpheus could call back the shade of a wife
By trusting and tuning the strings of his Thracian lyre,
If Pollux could win back a brother by taking the road
Repeatedly in and out of the land of the dead,
If Theseus and Hercules too . . . But why speak of them?
I myself am of highest birth, a descendant of Jove.'   170

He was praying like that and holding on to the altar
When the Sibyl started to speak: 'Blood relation
Of gods, Trojan, son of Anchises,
It is easy to descend into Avernus.
Death's dark door stands open day and night.
But to retrace your steps and get back to upper air,
That is the task, that is the undertaking.
Only a few have prevailed, sons of gods

Whom Jupiter favoured, or heroes exalted to glory
By their own worth. At the centre it is all forest   180
And a ring of dark waters, the river Cocytus, furls
And flows round it. Still, if love so torments you,
If your need to be ferried twice across the Styx
And twice to explore that deep dark abyss
Is so overwhelming, if you will and must go
That far, understand what else you must do.
Hid in the thick of a tree is a golden bough,
Gold to the tips of its leaves and the base of its stem,
Sacred (tradition declares) to the queen of that place.
It is safe there, roofed in by forests, in the pathless   190
Shadowy valleys. No one is ever allowed
Down to earth's hidden places unless he has first
Plucked this sprout of fledged gold from its tree
And handed it over to fair Proserpina
To whom it belongs, by decree, her own special gift.
And when it is plucked, a second one grows every time
In its place, golden again, emanating
That same sheen and shimmer. Therefore look up
And search deep, and as soon as you find it
Take hold of it boldly and duly. If fate has called you,   200
The bough will come away in your hand.
Otherwise, no strength you muster will break it,
Nor the hardest forged blade lop it off.

'But while you linger here on my doorstep,
Consulting and suing, sad news, alas,

Awaits: the body of one of your friends
Lies emptied of life, and his death pollutes
The whole fleet. Carry this man to a right
Resting place, lay him into his tomb,
Sacrifice herds of black sheep as your first   210
Votive offerings. Then and then only
Will you view the forests of Styx, those realms
Barred to the living.' She said these things,
Pressed her lips shut, and went silent.

Aeneas, his face sadder now, looking downcast,
Walked away from the cave, not sure what to think
Or expect. Trusty Achates walked at his side,
In step with his friend, apprehensive,
Intense, the give and take of their talk
Uncertain yet urgent: who, for example, might be   220
The dead comrade the Sibyl enjoined them
To bury? And then they saw him, Misenus,
On a dry stretch of beach – they came up and saw
The son of Aeolus, unfairly, peremptorily
Called to his death, this man unsurpassed
At rallying fighters, blaring the war call
On his bronze trumpet. Once he had been
Great Hector's comrade, standing by him in battle,
Unmistakable, known by his trumpet and spear.
Then after Achilles had savaged Hector to death   230
This staunchest of heroes, unwilling to join
A less worthy cause, chose to follow Aeneas.

But a mad moment came when the trumpeter blew
Resonant notes from a conch shell over the waves,
Intending to challenge the gods
To a musical contest. Triton was shaken
With envy (hard as it is to believe) and surged up
And drowned him in a sudden backwash of foam.

So the Trojans assembled and lifted their voices
In mourning, none louder, more devout than Aeneas;   240
Then, still in tears, they set to at once, eager
To follow the Sibyl's instruction, piling up logs,
Building an altar-pyre that rose toward the heavens.
High in the virgin forest, near dens of wild beasts,
Holm oaks echo the crack of their axes, spruce trees
Get felled, they hammer in wedges, split open
Beams of the ash and the tougher cross-grain of oak.
Big rowan trees crash and roll from the hilltop down.

As all this proceeded, Aeneas was to the fore,
Geared out like the rest, cheering everyone on.   250
But he kept gazing up at that high stretch of forest,
Sadly preoccupied, pondering things in his heart
Until a prayer rose to his lips and he said:
'If only that golden bough would show itself
On its tree in the deep forest den – for everything
The prophetess said about you, Misenus, was true,
Altogether too true!' And almost immediately
A pair of doves chanced down from the sky

In full view, and settled on the green grass;
In them the great hero knew his own mother's birds   260
And prayed and rejoiced: 'O, if a way can be found.
Be you my guides. Hold course through the air,
Lead on to the grove where that opulent bough
Overshadows the rich forest floor. And you,
O my goddess mother, do not abandon me
In this time of confusion.' With that he halted
To watch for what signs they might give, what place
They might make for. But the doves kept on going,
Now feeding, now flying ahead, at all times
Staying in view of the eyes that pursued them.   270

Then when they came to the fuming gorge at Avernus
They swept up through clear air and back down
To their chosen perch, a tree that was two trees
In one, green-leafed yet refulgent with gold.
Like mistletoe shining in cold winter woods,
Gripping its tree but not grafted, always in leaf,
Its yellowy berries in sprays curled round the bole –
Those flickering gold tendrils lit up the dark
Overhang of the oak and chimed in the breeze.
There and then Aeneas took hold of the bough   280
And although it resisted greedily tore it off,
Then carried it back to the Sibyl's cavern.

On the beach the Trojans were mourning
Misenus as sorely as ever, paying

Their last respects to the inert ash.
With resinous pinewood and cut-off sections of oak
They constructed first a huge pyre, dressing its flanks
With branches darkly in leaf, fencing the base
With funereal cypress, crowning all
With resplendent armour and weapons. Some heated 290
Water in bubbling vats above open fires, washed
And anointed the corpse, then raised the lament.
Next, when the weeping was over, they laid him out
On the ritual couch, his remains swathed in purple,
Familiar robes of the dead. Some stepped in
To lift high the great bier – a grievous observance –
And with eyes averted, as ancestral custom required,
Touched a blazing torch to the base of the pyre.
Gifts of food, piled offerings, incense, and bowls
Brimming over with oil went up in the flames. 300
Then when the fire had died, collapsing to ash,
They poured wine on his parched dust; and Corynaeus
Collected the bones in a bronze urn and sealed them.
Three times he moved round the company, sprinkling
Clean water for purification, asperging men lightly
From an olive branch, dewy with promise; then gave
The farewell. And under a high airy hill
Aeneas reared a magnificent tomb
Hung with the dead man's equipment, his oar
And his trumpet, so the hill is now called 310
Misenus, a name that will live down the ages.

Once this was done, Aeneas quickly proceeded
To follow the Sibyl's instructions. There was a cave,
A deep rough-walled cleft, stone jaws agape
Above a dark lake, with the lake and a grove
For protection and shelter. No creature of air
Could wing its way safely over that water,
Such were the noxious fumes spewing up
From the murky chasm into the vault of the heavens.
(The Greeks therefore called it Avernus, 'place   320
Without birds').
                    The first thing the priestess did here
Was line up four black heifers, pour libations of wine
On their foreheads, clip off the bristles that sprouted
Between their horns and commence sacrifice,
Offering them on the flames, all the while praying
Her clamorous prayers to Hecate, she who has power
Under the earth and above it. Others draw blades,
Catching warm blood in vessels. Aeneas himself
With a stroke of his sword, to honour Dark Night   330
And her sister, the Earth, slays a black-fleeced lamb,
And to honour you, Proserpina, a heifer,
Infertile. Then for the King of the Underworld
He illumines the dark, consecrating an altar
Where he burns whole carcasses and pours
Sluggish oil on the glowing entrails of bulls.
But all of a sudden, between the first glimmer
And full rise of the sun, the ground at their feet
Starts rumbling and shaking, the wooded heights

Are atremble, and in the uncanny light what they hear   340
Sounds like the howling of dogs as Hecate approaches.
'Out from here,' the seeress is shouting, 'out,
Anyone here not initiate – all such,
Depart from the grove. But not you, Aeneas:
Take you the sword from your scabbard, go ahead
On the road. Now will spirit be tested,
Now, now your courage must hold.' So saying, rapt
And unstoppable, she hurled herself into the mouth
Of the wide-open cave, and he, without fear,
Kept in step as she guided him forward.   350

Gods who rule over souls! Shades who subsist
In the silence! Chaos and Phlegethon, O you hushed
Nocturnal expanses, let assent be forthcoming
As I tell what's been given to tell, let assent be divine
As I unveil things profoundly beyond us,
Mysteries and truths buried under the earth.

On they went then in darkness, through the lonely
Shadowing night, a nowhere of deserted dwellings,
Dim phantasmal reaches where Pluto is king –
Like following a forest path by the hovering light   360
Of a moon that clouds and unclouds at Jupiter's whim,
While the colours of the world pall in the gloom.

In front of the house of the dead,
Between its dread jambs, is a courtyard where pain

And self-wounding thoughts have ensconced themelves.
Here too are pallid diseases, the sorrows of age,
Hunger that drives men to crime, agonies of the mind,
Poverty that demeans – all of these haunting nightmares
Have their beds in the niches. Death too, and sleep,
The brother of death, and terror, and guilty pleasures   370
That memory battens on. Also close by that doorway:
The iron cells of the Furies, death-dealing War
And fanatical Violence, her viper-tresses astream
In a bloodstained tangle of ribbons.
                                                    Right in the middle
Stands an elm, copious, darkly aflutter, old branches
Spread wide like arms, and here, it is said,
False dreams come to roost, clinging together
On the undersides of the leaves. At the gates,
Monstrosities brood in their pens, bewildering beasts   380
Of every form and description: two-natured Centaurs
And Scyllas, hundred-headed Briareus, the beast of Lerna,
Loathsome and hissing, and fire-fanged Chimaera;
Gorgons and Harpies too, and the looming menace
Of triple-framed Geryon. Faced with this rout,
Aeneas is thrown into panic, pulls out his sword,
Swings it round in defence, and had not his guide
In her wisdom forewarned him
That these were lives without substance, phantoms,
Apparitional forms, he would have charged   390
And tried to draw blood from shadows.

17

A road starts here that leads to Acheron river.
Here too is the roiling abyss, heaving with mud,
Venting a silty upsurge into Cocytus,
And beside these flowing streams and flooded wastes
A ferryman keeps watch, surly, filthy and bedraggled
Charon. His chin is bearded with unclean white shag;
The eyes stand in his head and glow; a grimy cloak
Flaps out from a knot tied at the shoulder.
All by himself he poles the boat, hoists sail   400
And ferries dead souls in his rusted craft,
Old but still a god, and in a god old age
Is green and hardy.
                    Hereabouts a crowd
Came pouring to the banks, women and men,
And noble-minded heroes separated now
From their living flesh, young boys, unmarried girls,
And sons cremated before their fathers' eyes:
Continuous as the streaming leaves nipped off
By first frost in the autumn woods, or flocks of birds   410
Blown inland from the stormy ocean, when the year
Turns cold and drives them to migrate
To countries in the sun. There they stood, those souls,
Begging to be the first allowed across, stretching out
Arms that hankered towards the farther shore.
The stern boatman permits one group to board
And now another, but the rest he denies passage,
Driving them back, away from the sandy banks.

Amazed and then moved by all this press and pleading,
Aeneas asks his guide: 'What does it mean, O Sibyl,   420
This push to the riverbank? What do these souls desire?
What decides that one group is held back, another
Rowed across the muddy waters?'

                              'Son of Anchises,'
The venerable one replied, 'O true born son of heaven,
What you see here are the standing pools
Of Cocytus and the Stygian marsh.
These are the names invoked when gods swear oaths
They will never dare to break. That crowd in front of you
Died but were left unburied, with no help or hope.
The ferryman is Charon. The ones on board his craft   431
Are the buried. Not until bones have found a last
Resting place will shades be let across
These gurgling currents, their doom instead to wander
And haunt about the banks for a hundred years.
Then and then only are they again allowed
To approach the brink and waters that they long for.'

Aeneas stopped and stood there, lost in thought,
Comprehending, pity in his heart
At their misfortune, then caught sight of Leucaspis   440
And Orontes, who'd captained the Lycian fleet,
Downcast men, denied the rites of the dead:
On their journey out from Troy, a southern gale
Struck ship and crew in heavy seas, and both
Were swept away, overwhelmed in the turmoil.

And now there appears his helmsman, Palinurus,
Who not long since had pitched and tumbled off
The stern into open sea, as he held course
From Africa, eyes fixed upon the stars.
To whom Aeneas, once he recognised   450
His sad form in the congregating dark,
Spoke first: 'Which god snatched you from us,
Palinurus, and drowned you in the deep?
Tell, O tell what happened. Never until now
Did Apollo's oracle prove false, but this time
He deceived me: you would survive the waves,
He prophesied, and land safe on the shore
Of Italia. Is this how he keeps his word?'
But Palinurus answered, 'My captain, son
Of Anchises, the god Apollo's oracle   460
Did not play you false, nor did any god
Plunge me into the waves. What happened was this:
The steering oar I held and was in charge of
Snapped in a sudden gale and as I fell
I dragged it down with me. But I swear by Ocean
The fear I had for myself then was as nothing
To the fear I had for your ship.
Stripped of her tackle, her steersman overboard,
Would she not wallow and founder
In those mountainous seas? For three nights,   470
Through horizonless surge, a south wind
Hurled me and burled me. The fourth day at dawn,
I rose on a swell and got my first glimpse

20

Of Italia. Little by little then I was making headway,
Slugging towards land in my waterlogged clothes,
Getting a grip on the razor-backed ridges,
When savage locals appeared with drawn swords,
A pack who for want of knowing assumed
That I'd be rich pickings. Now surf keeps me dandled,
The shore winds loll me and roll me.   480

You, therefore, you the unbowed, the unbroken,
I implore, by the cheerful light of the sky
And its breezes, by your father and your hopes
As the father of Iulus, get me away
From this place, put an end to my woes.
Either scatter the handful of earth
On my corpse, which you easily can
Once you're back in the harbour at Velia,
Or else – if there be a way, if your goddess-mother
Can direct you to one – for I believe you are bound   490
To enjoy the favour of heaven, prepared as you are
To face these vast waterways and set sail
On the Stygian marsh – reach out your hand
To one who is suffering, take me with you
Over the waves, so that in death at the least
I shall find a calm haven.'
                              That was his plea
To Aeneas, and this was the answer he got
From the Sibyl: 'What madness is this, Palinurus?
You who aren't even buried, what makes you think   500

You can look on the waters of Styx or the Furies'
Grim river? You have not been called to the bank.
Banish the thought that praying can ever affect
The edicts of gods. Your plight is a hard one,
But hear and remember my words: they should be
A comfort. What will happen is this:
Your bones will be reverenced; the sky
Will reveal signs and portents, in cities
On every side populations will know
To build you a tomb and observe solemn custom   510
With offerings year after year. And the place
For all time will bear the name Palinurus.'
These words lifted his heart and raised,
For a moment, his spirits. The thought
Of the land in his name makes him happy.

So now they resumed their journey and kept going
Until they were near the river, moving through
Silent woodland towards the bank, when Charon
From his boat out on the water spied them
And began to remonstrate, on the attack   520
Before they even spoke: 'You, whoever you are,
Approaching our river under arms, stop there,
Not one step farther, and say what brings you:
This is the country of the shades, of heavy-lidded
Night and sleep. It is a thing forbidden
To load the Stygian ferry with living bodies.
I rue the day I carried Hercules

And Theseus and Pirithous, sons of gods as they were,
Strongmen, invincibles. Hercules arrived
To chain up and restrain the hellmouth watchdog, 530
To steal him from the very throne of the king –
And did carry the panicked beast away. The others
Tried to abduct the queen from Pluto's bed.'
To which the soothsaying priestess made reply:
'Nothing like that is being plotted here. These arms
And weapons present you with no threat, so be calm.
Let the monster cave-dog howl his howl forever
And keep on terrifying bloodless shades,
Proserpina be her pure self behind her uncle's doors.
Aeneas of Troy, renowned for his right life 540
And warrior prowess, descends among the shades,
Down to death's deepest regions, to see his father.
If the sight of such devotedness won't move you,
You nevertheless must recognise this bough,'
And she shows the bough concealed by her cloak.
Charon quietens then, his bad temper subsides,
He says no more. It is long since he beheld
The holy proffer of that fateful branch. He turns
His dark barge round and steers for the shore.
Other souls ensconced on the long thwarts 550
He hurries off up gangways, then at once
Hands mighty Aeneas down into the vessel.
Under that weight the boat's plied timbers groan
And thick marsh water oozes through the leaks,
But in the end it is a safe crossing, and he lands

23

Soldier and soothsayer on slithery mud, knee-deep
In grey-green sedge.

                Here Cerberus keeps watch,
Growling from three gullets, his brute bulk couched
In the cave, facing down all comers. But the Sibyl,   560
Seeing snake-hackles bristle on his necks,
Flings him a dumpling of soporific honey
And heavily drugged grain. The ravenous triple maw
Yawns open, snaffles the sop it has been thrown
Until next thing the enormous flanks go slack
And the inert form slumps to the cave floor.
Thus, with the watchdog sunk in a deep sleep,
Aeneas gains entry and is quick to put behind him
The bank of that river none comes back across.

At once a sound of crying fills the air, the high wails   570
And weeping of infant souls, little ones denied
Their share of sweet life, torn from the breast
On life's very doorstep. A dark day bore them off
And sank them in untimely death. Next to them
Are those condemned to death on false charges,
Although here they are assigned their proper verdicts
By a rightly chosen jury. Minos, the judge,
Presides and shakes the urn, convenes a panel
Of the silent dead, seeking to establish
Men's characters and crimes. Farther on   580
Is the dwelling place of those unhappy spirits
Who died by their own hand, simply driven

By life to a fierce rejection of the light.
How they long now for the open air above,
How willingly they would endure the lot
Of exhausted workers and the hard-wrought poor.
But their way is barred by laws of gods. The waste
And desolate marsh water laps round,
River Styx with its nine loops binds and bounds them.

Not far from here the fields called the Fields 590
Of Mourning stretch out in all directions.
On these plains, hidden on shadowy paths,
Secluded and embowered in myrtle groves,
Are those who suffered hard and cruel decline
In thrall to an unremitting love. Their griefs
Do not relent, not even in death. Here Aeneas saw
Among other lovers Phaedra and Procris,
And sad Eriphyle, pointing to the wounds
Dealt by her callous son. Evadne too,
And Pasiphaë. And moving in step with them 600
Laodamia, and Caeneus who in her time had known
Life as a man, though fate had now restored
The figure of the woman she once was.

Along with these, still nursing her raw wound,
Dido of Carthage strayed in the great forest.
As soon as the Trojan came close and made out
Her dimly wavering form among the shadows,
He was like one who sees or imagines he has seen

A new moon rising up among the clouds
On the first day of the month; there and then
He wept and spoke these loving, tender words:
'Unhappy Dido! So the news I got was true,
That you had left the world, had taken a sword
And bade your last farewell. Was I, O was I to blame
For your death? I swear by the stars, by the powers
Above and by any truth there may be under earth,
I embarked from your shore, my queen, unwillingly.
Orders from the gods, which compel me now
To travel among shades in this mouldering world,
This bottomless pit of night, dictated
Obedience then as well. How could I believe
My going would devastate you with such grief?
Stay a moment, don't slip out of our sight.
Is there someone you are trying to avoid?
These words I'm saying to you are the last
Fate will permit me, ever.'
                          Pleading like this,
Tears welling up inside him, Aeneas tried
To placate her fiery spirit and soften
Her fierce gaze; but she, averting her face,
Her eyes fixed steadily on the ground, turned
And showed no sign of having heard, no more
Than if her features had been carved in flint
Or Parian marble. At length she swept away
And fled, implacable, into the dappling shadows
Of the grove, where Sychaeus, her husband

In another earlier time, feels for her pain
And reciprocates the love she bears him still;
While Aeneas, no less stricken by the injustice
Of her fate, gazes into the distance after her,   640
Gazes through tears, and pities her as she goes.

Then he braces himself for the journey still to come
And soon they arrive in the farthest outlying fields,
The hosting grounds of those renowned in war.
In one place Tydeus meets him, in another
Parthenopaeus, glorious in arms, and the bloodless
Shade of Adrastus; elsewhere the Trojan chieftains
Who fell in battle, much mourned in the world above.
And now he also moaned to see them
Thronging in such numbers: Glaucus, Medon   650
And Thersilochus, Antenor's three sons; Polyboetes,
The priest of Ceres; and Idaeus, still
The chariot driver, still dressed in his armour.
From right and left souls crowd and jostle close,
Eager for more than just a look at him; they want
His company, the joy of keeping in step, talking,
Learning why he has come. But the Greek captains
And the gleaming cohorts once led by Agamemnon
Cowered in panic when they saw Aeneas
Advance in dazzling armour through the gloom.   660
Some turned to flee as they had once to the ships,
Some raised a spectral cry that came to nothing,
Dying away as it left their gaping mouths.

27

And here Aeneas caught sight of Priam's son,
Deiphobus, mutilated in every part, his face
In shreds – his face and his two hands –
Ears torn from his head, and his nostrils
(A low dishonourable wounding, this)
His nostrils cut away: unrecognisable almost
As he shivered and shrank into himself to hide   670
The cruel laceration. Aeneas,
In a voice well known to him, spoke first, resolutely:
'Deiphobus, mightiest in the field, offspring
Of Teucer's ancient line, who was there capable
Of such mutilation? Who let themselves
Run so ruthlessly amok? The story I heard was this:
On the last night in Troy, you waded in Greek blood
Till you fell exhausted, fell like a dead man
On a heap of their slobbered corpses. That is why
I raised an empty tomb for you at Rhoetum,   680
On the shore, and with my three loud cries
Invoked your spirit. Your name now and your arms
Hallow that spot. But not you in the flesh, my friend,
Whom I could neither see as I embarked
Nor bury in home ground.'
                              Priam's son replied:
'And you, my friend, you left no thing undone.
You paid the right attention to Deiphobus,
Dead man and shade. It was my destiny
And the criminal, widowing schemes of my lady   690
Of Sparta wrecked and ruined me. What you see

28

Are the love bites she left me in remembrance
Of that last night, of all our city's nights
The most jubilant and most deluded. But this you know
Too well already, for how could you forget?
When the horse that was our fate came at a leap
On to the heights of Troy, big in the belly
With armed men, she was to the fore, involved
In the dance, contriving to lead our women
In the loud frenzy of the bacchanal.   700
Up she went to our citadel, in her hand
A torch conspicuously ablaze,
Signalling to the Greeks. And me then! Me
In my god-cursed marriage-bed, lying dead beat,
Far gone, giving in to sleep, sweet, welcoming,
Drowsy sleep, serene almost as death. Meanwhile,
My paragon of a bride had cleared the house
Of every weapon and even stolen the sword
From underneath my head; and now she opened doors
And called for Menelaus to come in, hoping, no doubt,   710
That this grand favour to her lover boy
Would blot out memories of old betrayals.
But why say more? They broke into the bedroom,
Ulysses with them, the insidious and malignant . . .
O gods, as my plea for vengeance is a just one. Gods!
Retaliate! Strike the Greeks with all due punishment.
But you, what of you? It is time I heard your story:
What turn of events has brought you here alive?
Do you come as a survivor, tempest-tossed,

29

Or at the gods' behest? What destiny hounds you   720
Down to these sunless, poor abodes, this land
Of troubles?'

        Dawn in her rose-flushed chariot
Had taken her airy drive up half the sky
As they talked together, and in all likelihood
They would have talked on for whatever time
Had been allotted, but that the Sibyl at Aeneas' side
Reproved him in a few brief words. 'Night, Aeneas,
Has begun to fall. We are wasting time lamenting.
This is the fork of the road, here it divides.   730
To the right, where it runs beneath the walls
Of mighty Pluto's fortress, that one we take
To Elysium; the one to the left sends evil-doers
To punishment in merciless Tartarus.'
                  Deiphobus
Then replied, 'Do not, high priestess, be angry.
I will be gone, will take my place with the rest, yield
Once more to the dark. But you, the glory of Troy, go,
Go you to a happier fate.'
            He had said   740
His say, and as he spoke turned on his heel.

Aeneas suddenly looks back and sees
A broad-based fortress under a cliff to the left,
Set behind three rings of wall, encircled
By a hurtling torrent, a surge and rush of flame,

Rock-rumbling, thunder-flowing Phlegethon, the fiery
Bourne of Tartarus. A gate rears up in front,
Flanked by pillars of solid adamant, so massive
No human force, nor even the sky-gods' squadrons
Could dislodge them. There too stands an iron tower   750
And from its top Tisiphone the Fury
Oversees the entrance day and night, unsleeping
And on guard, her bloody dress hitched up.
Sounds of groaning could be heard inside, the savage
Application of the lash, the fling and scringe and drag
Of iron chains. Aeneas stopped short, petrified,
Taking in the turmoil and the shouting,
Then asked the Sibyl: 'What wrong-doing
Is being dealt with here? What punishments
Afflict the wrong-doers? What is this wailing   760
High upon the wind?'
                And the prophetess
Answered him: 'Famed chieftain of the Trojans,
Know it is forbidden for the pure in spirit
To set foot on the god-cursed threshold. And yet
When Hecate gave me charge of Avernus' woods
She took me through this whole place and explained
The punishments gods impose. Rhadamanthus
Of Knossos rules here, unforgiving, castigating,
Hearing admissions of guilt and exacting   770
Confession from those self-deceiving souls
Who thought to hide wrongs done in the world above
And left them unatoned for till too late.

Vengeful Tisiphone keeps bearing down, a whiplash
Lapped and lithe in her right hand, in her left
A flail of writhing snakes, scourging the guilty,
Summoning her ferocious claque of sisters.
Next comes a grinding scrunch and screech
Of hinges as the dread doors open
And you see what waits inside, the shape   780
And threat of the guard who haunts the threshold.
Farther in and more ruthless still, the Hydra lurks,
Monstrous, with her fifty gaping mouth-holes
And black gullets. And beyond, the sheer plunge
Of Tartarus down to the depths, to darkness, a drop
Twice as far beneath the earth as Olympus
Appears to soar above it.
                              In the bottom of the pit,
In the very lowest sump, felled by Jove's thunderbolt,
Earth's ancient sons, the Titans, writhe, abased.   790
Here too I saw the sons of Aloeus, giant twins
Who attempted to grapple with high heaven
And depose the Father of the Skies.
Salmoneus too I saw, paying dear
For having played at being Jupiter, wielding fire
And imitating the thunders of Olympus.
He rode in triumph through the Greek nations
And his own city in Elis, drawn by four horses
And flourishing a torch, assuming to himself
The honour due to gods. It was madness: 800
To think that the batter of bronze and the clatter

Of horses' hoofs could mimic Jupiter's
Absolute thunder and his scowling storms!
But the all-powerful Father – no fake lightning for him
From torches or smoky guttering pine-brands –
Hurled his bright bolt from behind the cloud murk
And blasted Salmoneus headlong down
In an overwhelming whirlwind. There as well
You'd see Tityos, foster-son of Earth,
The mother of all. Tityos, his body stretching out   810
Over nine whole acres while a huge, horrendous
Vulture puddles forever with hooked beak
In his liver and entrails teeming with raw pain.
It burrows deep below the breastbone, feeding
And foraging without respite, for the gnawed-at
Gut and gutstrings keep renewing.
                                        And the Lapiths,
Ixion and Parothous, should I mention them?
Eternally menaced by a looming boulder, black
And eternally about to fall. Golden headrests   820
Gleam on their high banquet couches, a sumptuous
Royal feast is spread to tempt them; but nearby
The arch-Fury occupies her place, warding off
Hands that long to reach out to the meal, ever ready
To spring, with her lifted torch and terrifying yells.

'Also incarcerated, those who for a lifetime
Hated a brother, abused a parent, or ruined
The good name of a client; those who gloated

On wealth they'd secretly amassed and hoarded
And failed to share with kith and kin (they comprised   830
The biggest crowd); those killed as adulterers;
Those who broke oaths of loyalty to masters
In violent rebellions: all were confined there
Awaiting punishment. What that punishment would be,
What fault or fate entailed it, do not seek to know.
Some roll a massive boulder or hang spreadeagled,
Tied to the spokes of wheels. Theseus, unlucky soul,
Sits unmoving and will sit like that forever,
While Phlegyas, most stricken of all, cautions all,
A constant proof of what his voice proclaims   840
Loudly through the darkness: "Take warning by me;
Learn to do right; learn not to scorn the gods."
Here too was one who sold his country's freedom,
Leaving her in thrall to a tyrant lord;
Here one who would fix laws for a price and for a price
Unfix them; here another who forced a daughter
In her bed and into an abominable marriage.
All dared to commit great wrong and were fit
For what they dared. If I had a hundred tongues,
If I had a hundred mouths and an iron voice,   850
I could neither spell out the foul catalogue
Of those crimes nor name their punishments.'

Here Apollo's venerable priestess paused
Before continuing: 'But enough. Be quick. You must
Conclude your undertaking now. We both must hurry.

I see ramparts fashioned in Cyclopic foundries
And gates there in the arch in front of us
Where the powers that be require us to deposit
Proserpina's gift.' That said, they proceed in step
Along the dark of pathways, then hurry out   860
Across the open ground that fronts the doors.
Aeneas takes his stand in the entrance, purifies
His body with fresh water, and there and then
Plants the bough in the threshold.

                               With this ritual
Finally performed and honour done to the goddess,
They came into happy vistas and the green welcome
Of the Groves of the Fortunate Ones who dwell in joy.
Here a more spacious air sheds brightness
Over the land; they enjoy their own sun here   870
And their own stars – some at their exercises
On the grass, some competing in earnest, wrestling
On yellow sand; others are dancing dances
And singing songs, Orpheus among them
In his long musician's robe, keeping time,
Plucking his seven notes from the seven-stringed lyre
Now with his fingers, now with an ivory plectrum.
Here too were members of Teucer's ancient stock,
That noblest of families, magnificent heroes
Born in better days – Illus and Assaracus   880
And Dardanus who founded Troy. Aeneas gazed
In wonder at their armour and the chariots beside them

35

Standing idle, their spears struck tall in the ground
And their horses loosed out, free to graze the plain
Anywhere they liked. The pride they took when alive
In armour and chariots, the care they gave
To their glossy well-groomed teams, it is still the same
Now they have gone away under the earth. Others too
He sees on every side, feasting in lush meadows
Or singing songs together to Apollo   890
Deep in a laurel grove, where the Eridanus
Courses through on its way to the earth above.

Here was a band of those who suffered wounds
Fighting for their country; those who lived the pure life
Of the priest; those who were dedicated poets
And made songs fit for Apollo; others still
Whose discoveries improved our arts or ease, and those
Remembered for a life spent serving others –
All of them with headbands white as snow
Tied round their brows. These the Sibyl now addressed
As they bustled close around her, Musaeus   901
In particular, who stood out at the centre of the crowd,
The one looked up to, towering head and shoulders
Over them. 'Tell us, happy spirits,' she began,
'And you, the best of the poets, tell us
Where does Anchises lodge, in which quarter?
For his sake we have crossed the mighty waterways
To be here.' Her question the great hero answered
Briefly: 'None of us has one definite home place.

We haunt the shadowy woods, bed down on riverbanks,
On meadowland in earshot of running streams.   911
But you, if your heart is set upon it, climb this ridge
And I'll direct you soon on an easy path.' He spoke,
Walked on ahead and showed the fields of light.
Aeneas and the Sibyl came down the hill.

                                     Elsewhere Anchises,
Fatherly and intent, was off in a deep green valley
Surveying and reviewing souls consigned there,
Those due to pass to the light of the upper world.
It so happened he was just then taking note   920
Of his whole posterity, the destinies and doings,
Traits and qualities of descendants dear to him,
But seeing Aeneas come wading through the grass
Towards him, he reached his two hands out
In eager joy, his eyes filled up with tears
And he gave a cry: 'At last! Are you here at last?
I always trusted that your sense of right
Would prevail and keep you going to the end.
And am I now allowed to see your face,
My son, and hear you talk, and talk to you myself?   930
This is what I imagined and looked forward to
As I counted the days; and my trust was not misplaced.
To think of the lands and the outlying seas
You have crossed, my son, to receive this welcome.
And after such dangers! I was afraid that Africa
Might be your undoing.' But Aeneas replied:
'Often and often, father, you would appear to me,

Your sad shade would appear, and that kept me going
To this end. My ships are anchored in the Tuscan sea.
Let me take your hand, my father, O let me, and do not   940
Hold back from my embrace.' And as he spoke he wept.
Three times he tried to reach arms round that neck.
Three times the form, reached for in vain, escaped
Like a breeze between his hands, a dream on wings.

Meanwhile, at the far end of a valley, Aeneas saw
A remote grove, bushy rustling thickets,
And the river Lethe somnolently flowing,
Lapping those peaceful haunts along its banks.
Here a hovering multitude, innumerable
Nations and gathered clans, kept the fields   950
Humming with life, like bees in meadows
On a clear summer day alighting on pied flowers
And wafting in mazy swarms around white lilies.
Aeneas startled at this unexpected sight
And in his bewilderment asked what was happening,
What was the river drifting past beyond them,
Who were the ones in such a populous throng
Beside it?
            'Spirits,' Anchises answered,
'They are spirits destined to live a second life   960
In the body; they assemble here to drink
From the brimming Lethe, and its water
Heals their anxieties and obliterates
All trace of memory. For a long time now

I have looked forward to telling you about them,
Letting you see them face to face, but most of all
I wished to call the roll of my descendants, parade
My children's children, so you could all the more
Share my joy at your landfall in Italia.'

'Are we to believe then, father, there are souls   970
Who rise from here to the sky of the upper world
And re-enter the sluggish drag of the body?
What possesses the poor souls? Why this mad desire
To get back to the light?' 'To put you out of doubt,'
Anchises answers, 'I shall explain it straightaway.'
And point by point he then outlines the doctrine.

'To begin at the beginning: a nurturing inner spirit
Works to sustain sky, earth, the fields of ocean,
The moon's bright disc and Titan's star, the sun;
And mind, operative in every part, imbues   980
The massive whole, blending with world's body.
From which are born races of men and beasts,
Creatures that fly, and prodigies ocean breeds
Beneath the molten marble of its surface.
The seeds of life are strong sparks out of fire,
Their origin divine, so to that extent
They are immune to the heavy toll of the body,
Their quickness unaffected by the toil
Of human limbs and the mortal clothing
Of the flesh. It is from body   990

That fear and desire, grief and delight derive,
And in the darkness of its prison house
Those first pure elements are shut off and screened
From the light of heaven. Besides which, at the end
When life departs, they remain sadly infested
By every evil and every bodily ill,
For inevitably, in the course of time,
Many flaws mysteriously coalesce, hard set
And deep ingrained. Therefore souls are visited
With due chastisements and affliction, to atone   1000
For past offences. Some are hung racked
And raked by vacuous winds; for others, the stain
Is washed away beneath whirling torrents
Or burnt off in fire. Each of us suffers
The death we're due, then given the freedom
Of broad Elysium – the few, that is, who'll dwell
In those blessèd fields until the end of time
When length of days will remove the deep-dyed taint,
Purify the aethereal sense and that sheer original stuff
Of fire and spirit. The rest, when they have trod   1010
Time's mill for a thousand years, the god commands
Wave upon wave into the Lethe river, so at that stage
Their memory is effaced and they go once more
To dwell beneath sky's dome and start again
To long for the old life of flesh and blood.'

Anchises concluded and led his son
Accompanied by the Sibyl into the crowd,

Into the thick and buzzing throb of it,
Then took his stand on a height where he could inspect
The long, drawn-out procession and take note   1020
Of every face as it approached and passed.

'So now I will instruct you in what is to be,
The future glory of the Trojan race,
Descendants due to be born in Italia,
Souls who in time will make our name illustrious –
I speak of them to reveal your destiny to you.
The lad you see there, who leans on his untipped spear,
Placed next and nearest to the light, he will be
The first to ascend to upper air, the first
Of our people with mixed Italian blood.   1030
He'll be known as Silvius, an Alban name,
And be the last of your children; when you are old
Your wife Lavinia will rear him in the woods
To be a king and to father kings our stock
Will issue from and rule in Alba Longa.
Next to him stands Procas, pride and joy
Of the Trojan nation, then Capys and Numitor
And the one in whose name you will survive, Silvius
Aeneas, no less distinguished as a warrior than you
And no less devoted, though he'll be waiting long   1040
To rule in Alba. Look at them! Marvellous, strong
Young men, wearing their civic honours, oak wreaths
Like shadowy crowns. These, when you are gone,
Will build Nomentum and Gabii and the city of Fidena,

41

Fortify hill towns, wall the citadels
Of Collatia, found Pometii, Bola and Cora
And Camp Inuus: unheard-of today, unsignified,
Their name and fame will come. And Romulus, yes,
Son of Mars, grandson of Numitor, whom Illia
Is to bear, Romulus will stand firm by his grandfather.   1050
Do you see how the twin plumes wave above his head,
How the Father of the gods has marked him out
With his own insignia for singular majesty?
Once he inaugurates the power of Rome,
She in her glory will push an empire's bounds
To the ends of earth and harbour aspirations
High as heaven; seven hills she will girdle with a wall
Into a single city and be blessed with heroic sons.
She will be like Cybele with her crown of towers,
The Great Mother borne in her chariot   1060
Through the cities of Phrygia, happy and fulfilled
To have given birth to gods, grandchildren
By the score in her generous arms,
All of them sky-dwellers, tenants of the heights.

'Now look this way, take good note of this clan,
Your own bloodline in Rome: there is Caesar
And the whole offspring of Iulus, destined one day
To issue forth beneath the dome of heaven.
This is he whose coming you've heard foretold
So often: Augustus Caesar, child of the divine one,   1070
Who will establish in Latium, in Saturn's old domain,

42

A second golden age. He will advance his empire
Beyond the Garamants and the Indians
To lands unseen beneath our constellations
Beyond the sun's path through the zodiac,
Away where sky-braced Atlas pivots on his shoulder
The firmament, inlaid with glittering stars.
Already the Caspian kingdoms and Maeotia
Know of his coming and begin to tremble
At the oracles of their gods; the waters of the Nile   1080
Quail in alarm and roil through their seven mouths.
Not even Hercules pursued his labours over
So much of earth's surface, not when he stalked
And shot the bronze-toed deer, silenced the boar
In the woods of Erymanthus and left the air of Lerna
Vibrating to his bowstring; not Bacchus either
Careering in triumph, the vine-reins in his grip,
Driving his tiger team down the heights of Nysa.
So why should we then hesitate to test
And prove our worth in action or be afraid   1090
To stake and stand our ground in Italia?

'But that one in the crown of olive sprays,
Offering sacrifice – that grey head
And grizzled beard I recognise as Numa's,
King of Rome, sprung from the humble town
Of Cures, called from its poor land to wield high power
And frame the city's first system of laws.
To be succeeded next by Tullus, who will wreck

43

His country's peace, turn an easygoing people
Militant and drill an army long out of the field
For victory. After him, that's Ancus, swaggering,
Too full of himself already, overly susceptible
To the wind of popularity in his sails.
And there, if you care to look, are the regal Tarquins
And haughty Brutus, called Avenger, who'll arrange
The handover of the fasces – first consul
To be installed and given authority
As custodian of the pitiless axes.
Then as a father, when his sons foment their plot,
He will decree their summary execution
In the fair name of liberty – stricken in this
No matter how future generations may comprehend it:
Love of country will prevail and the overwhelming
Desire for fame.

       'Now over there you see
The Decii and the Drusi, Torquatus who will behead
His son, and Camillus who'll recapture the standards.
But alas for that pair in their burnished armour,
Well-matched champions, twin souls in accord
As long as they stay pent in this shadowland,
But once promoted to the light above
What mutual destruction they will wreak,
The internecine savagery and slaughter
Of a civil war: Caesar, the bride's father,
Bearing down from the northern Alps,

Pompey, the husband, with his legions in formation
Advancing from the east. Do not, O my sons,
Inure yourselves to such dreadful consequence, do not
Bloody the bosom of your country with vicious,
Valiant battle. And you, child of my blood,   1130
Of the gods on high Olympus, be you the first
In clemency: rid your hands of those weapons.

'Yonder too is Mummius, conqueror
Of Corinth, who will ride his victor's chariot
Up to the Capitol, a hero for having brought
Ruination on the Greeks. That other at his side
Will destroy Argos and Agamemnon's Mycenae,
Defeat descendants of arch-warrior Achilles,
Avenge his Trojan forebears and the rape
Of Cassandra in Minerva's temple.   1140
Next, great Cato, you, who could not sing your praise
Or, Cossus, yours? Or the family of the Gracchi;
Or those two Scipios, two warrior thunderbolts
Who will strike down bellicose Carthage; or Fabricius,
The indomitable and frugal; or you, Serranus,
Sowing your furrowed fields? Nor is there a quick
Or easy way to scan the long line of the Fabii,
Down to the greatest, Fabius Maximus,
He who'll contrive to stall and thereby save our state.
Others, I have no doubt, with a more delicate touch   1150
Will beat bronze into breathing likenesses,
Conjure living features out of marble,

Argue cases more effectively, and with their compass
Plot the heavens' orbit and predict
The rising of the constellations. But you, Roman,
Remember: to you will fall the exercise of power
Over the nations, and these will be your gifts –
To impose peace and justify your sway,
Spare those you conquer, crush those who overbear.'

Here Anchises paused; then, while they wondered   1160
At his words, continued: 'Look now, there goes
Marcellus, head and shoulders above all the rest,
Victorious in armour of the general he killed.
He will help Rome to stand firm while it bears the brunt
Of fierce invasion, he will ride high over
Carthiginians and insurgent Gauls, then dedicate
Those rich, rare spoils won only twice before
To Father Quirinus.'
                          At which point Aeneas saw
A young man in step with Marcellus, arrayed   1170
In glittering arms, exceedingly handsome
But with lowered eyes, unhappy looking, so he asked,
'Who, father, is that companion at his side?
A son, or another of his great descendants?
What crowds and clamour follow him! What presence
He has! But black night wreathes his brow
With dolorous shadow.'
                          Choking back his tears,
Anchises answered, 'Do not, O my son,

46

Seek foreknowledge of the heavy sorrow
Your people will endure. Fate will allow the world
Only to glimpse him, then rob it of him quickly.
It's as if the gods decided the Roman people
Would be manifestly too powerful, were the gift
Of his life to last. How the city will re-echo
Massed laments from the brave on the Field of Mars!
What a funeral procession, Tiber, you will witness
As you go flowing past the new built tomb!
No boy born from our Trojan stock will ever raise
The hopes of his Latin ancestors so high
Nor the land of Romulus take such pride in a son.
Alas for his goodness! His antique loyalties!
His strong right arm unbeaten in the battle!
No foe would have faced and fought him and survived,
Whether he marched on foot or sank his spurs
In the flanks of some foaming, lathering warhorse.
O son of pity! Alas that you cannot strike
Fate's cruel fetters off! For you are to be Marcellus . . .
Load my arms with lilies, let me scatter
Purple flowers, let me lavish these gifts at least
On the soul of my inheritor and perform
My unavailing duty.'
                          And so
Far and wide in those fields, through regions of air,
They go wandering at will, surveying all.
Then after Anchises has conducted Aeneas
Across the whole expanse, scene after scene,

And fired his mind with promise of future glory,
He tells of wars that will first have to be waged,
Of the Laurentines and the town of King Latinus,   1210
How he should face or flee each undertaking.

There are two gates of Sleep, one of which, they say,
Is made of horn and offers easy passage
To true visions; the other has a luminous, dense
Ivory sheen, but through it, to the sky above,
The spirits of the dead send up false dreams.
Anchises, still guiding and discoursing,
Escorts his son and the Sibyl on their way
And lets them both out by the ivory gate.
Aeneas hurries to the ships and rejoins his comrades,   1220
Then sails, hugging the shore, to the port of Caietae.
Anchors are cast from the prow; sterns cushion on sand.

Note on the Text

For the contemporary reader, it is the best of books and the worst of books. Best because of its mythopoeic visions, the twilit fetch of its language, the pathos of the many encounters it allows the living Aeneas with his familiar dead. Worst because of its imperial certitude, its celebration of Rome's manifest destiny and the catalogue of Roman heroes . . .

WITH THESE WORDS SEAMUS HEANEY began what he may have intended to serve as an afterword to *Aeneid* Book VI. Marked 'Katabasis, Eschatological' (the terms describe the final journey of the spirit into the underworld), it was the last element that he introduced to the text. He did not complete it and it remains a tantalising fragment; but he had, by then, completed a translation of Book VI in its entirety that, in July 2013, he marked 'final' in preparation for showing to his publisher. That typescript was still in his keeping on his death one month later. It contained two full-length drafts, as well as pages of rough working; and although one draft was clearly more advanced than the other, the presence of a second version made necessary the task of confirming that the work was indeed 'final' as Seamus intended. That search involved comparing a number of annotated and undated typescripts, as well as preliminary proofs for a limited, letterpress edition that he had been exploring with the Bonnefant Press in the Netherlands, in collaboration with the artist Jan Hendrix. From these documents and the accompanying correspondence, it has been possible to arrive at the text for this edition.

Seamus had largely settled the first 1064 lines of his translation by the time he saw a full-length letterpress proof from Bonnefant in 2011; that proof forms the basis of the text here, augmented by a small number of author amendments where they appeared as definitive instructions. The concluding sections of the poem, however – beyond line 1065 – continued to be reworked in typescript after that proof had been corrected, and it is for this reason that the last typescript becomes the preferred text from this point onward. The Translator's Note was prepared in two drafts of 2010.

This translation of 1222 lines is Seamus's complete rendering of Book VI: it follows the author's latest instructions, and contains no editorial interventions beyond the correction of literals. It seems likely that both poem and note would have received further revision had Seamus seen production through to completion, and in that respect, the author's use of the word 'final' may be considered a more precise description of the text than 'finished', as well as one in keeping with the Aeneid's own halted composition.

On behalf of the family and the publisher, our heartfelt gratitude extends to those trusted readers who advised Seamus on his translation, and to those who helped to assure us of the virtue of posthumous publication. Our thanks go also to the Bonnefant Press: to Jan Hendrix and publisher Hans van Eijk, for what Seamus described as 'an old friendship of artist, printer and poet'.

CATHERINE HEANEY

MATTHEW HOLLIS